The Battle of Gettysburg

(In poetry form)

George Trambukis

VANTAGE PRESS
New York

Cover design by Susan Thomas

FIRST EDITION

Published by Vantage Press, Inc.
516 West 34th Street, New York, New York 10001

Manufactured in the United States of America
ISBN: 0-533-14569-4

Library of Congress Catalog Card No.: 2003091685

0 9 8 7 6 5 4 3 2 1

To the brave men of both the North and the South who fought unselfishly for a cause they thought was right

Contents

Prologue

Lieutenant-General Thomas Jonathan Jackson (1824–1863)

(Sorely Missed at Gettysburg)

Jackson received his nickname "Stonewall" at the first
    battle of Bull Run,
As Brigadier General Bee was trying to rally his
    retreating men, who were overrun,
By shouting: "Yonder stands Jackson like a stone wall.
Let's rally to his defense"—it was a most prophetic call!
Henceforth Jackson was known as "Stonewall,"
And his brigade became the Stonewall brigade, known
    to all.
It formed a rallying point for the wavering rebel forces,
Who charged with fixed bayonets and stampeded the
    Yankees back with great losses.
That was the first of many actions in which Jackson, an
    ex-professor at Virginia Military Institute,
Gained a great victory for his outnumbered
    Confederates, which nobody can dispute!
He combined the qualities of a religious mystic with
    those of a warrior knight
And gained victory after victory with his daring insight.
In the Shenandoah Valley, with less than twenty
    thousand men,
He fought a half-dozen major battles, again and again,
Against armies three times his size and won each and
    every one.

Jackson marched with such incredible speed
His opponents dubbed his troops "Jackson's foot
    cavalry," who were always in the lead.
His men did more to defeat Union corps,
In 1862 and 1863, than any body of men in the entire
    war.
Jackson's masterpiece came at Chancellorsville,
Where defying every tenet of military science and skill,
He led an outnumbered army to victory and glory
In a flank attack and crushed Hooker's right wing and
    unsuspected quarry.
It ranks with Frederick the Great's maneuver at
    Leuthen,
As one of the greatest actions in martial record; barring
    none!
(Thousands of years ago, Alexander the Great used this
    flanking and oblique plot
To crush the Persians at the battles of Issus and Arbela,
    which King Darius led, the great Asiatic despot.)
While attempting to exploit his advantage and gain,
Jackson was mistakenly gunned down by his own men
    in the heat of the campaign.
Although his left arm was amputated,
He was expected to recover; but his health deteriorated.
Five days later he passed away,
Succumbing to pneumonia on Sunday, May 10, 1863, to
    everyone's dismay.
Professionally, Lee and Jackson meshed splendidly.
Lee would advise and aid, and Jackson would decide
    and execute rapidly.
With Lee planning and Jackson executing, the South
    had discovered a winning team.
Together they demonstrated true mastery of the art of
    war with high esteem.

'Twas like the hopes of all the South were lost
When "Stonewall" Jackson fell wounded off his horse.
It was a bad omen for the Southern men in gray,
To lose a general so daring, skillful and unafraid.
Hard and heavy must have been the heart of General
 Lee
To have lost a general who possessed so much audacity.
Slowly, up the Shenandoah Valley, Lee made his way
To rendezvous at Gettysburg, deprived of the one
 general who could have saved the day.
Lee sorely missed Jackson on the battlefield
Of Gettysburg for the decisiveness and aggressiveness
 that Jackson was wont to wield.
Would Jackson have hesitated, as Ewell did, in not
 attacking Cemetery and Culp's Hill,
Which were lightly fortified on the first day of battle,
 to complete the kill?
Would Jackson have hesitated when Lee ordered A. P.
 Hill a renewal of attack when he had the Union
 forces on the run,
And declined, saying his men were tired and needed
 rest, when the battle could have been won?
Would Jackson have dragged his feet as Longstreet had
 done
When ordered, on the second day, to attack at 10:00
 A.M., but only at noon was his attack begun?
Yes, as Lee said: "Jackson lost his left arm, but I have
 lost my right arm."
For the next two years, after the defeat at Gettysburg,
 Lee never won a victory with his command.
He was always on the defensive, with his gallant little
 band,
Always short of supplies, food, munitions, and always,
 always undermanned.

On Palm Sunday, April 9, 1865, with only thirteen
thousand men and sixty artillery pieces,
He surrendered at Appomattox Court House to General
Grant, and all resistance ceases.
Lee sorely missed "Stonewall" Jackson from his
command,
The religious mystic and fiery fire-brand.

The First Day

July 1, 1863

Ares, the God of war, from his perch on high,
The Southern and Northern armies does espy.
As General Lee slowly up the Shenandoah Valley made
    his way.
And General Hooker, on the other side of the Blue Ridge
    mountains, followed parallel the man in Gray.
General Lee, flushed with victory at Chancellorsville,
    the North decided to invade
And embarked, with high hopes, on this fatal crusade.
All day long up the Shenandoah Valley the beat of
    marching feet was heard,
And the dust rose to the high heavens and the sun
    almost disappeared.
For Robert E. Lee, it was an ominous day as he had lost,
At Chancellorsville, his most daring general: an
    unreplaceable loss.
General "Stonewall" Jackson was by his own men killed,
Having been mistaken for the enemy as darkness over
    all spilled.
He was returning to camp after successfully defeating
    the foe.
Thus, Lee was deprived of his most daring and
    imaginative general: a most devastating blow!
General Jackson's counsel and advice had been held in
    high esteem,
Especially by Lee, who now lost a most valued member
    of his team.

Major General Stuart, the commander of the cavalry,
and a most chivalrous fellow,
Decided to go around the Federal Troops and pursue his
own endeavor.
Thus, Stuart's cavalry, the eyes and ears of the South,
deprived Lee of valuable information,
And for eight days Lee was ignorant of Stuart's exact
position.
Lee divided his army under three commands,
Generals Longstreet, Ewell, and A.P. Hill, and was
satisfied that they were in good hands.
Ewell deep in Pennsylvania was sent on ahead,
Capturing the city of York and threatening a drive on
Harrisburg in search of supplies and bread.
General Hooker, in the meantime, lost his Union
command,
Being replaced by General Meade in hopes the Army of
the Potomac would be in steadier hands.
A.P. Hill and Longstreet were camped near Gettysburg,
east of Chambersburg,
And Early was well north of Gettysburg and on the road
to Harrisburg.
Union General Buford and his cavalry went on ahead
And entered the little town of Gettysburg with
apprehension and dread.
Meade ordered General Sickles's Third Corps to move
up
And ordered Reynolds's First Corps and Howard's
Eleventh Corps as a back-up.
Brigadier General Pettigrew had already entered
Gettysburg, looking for shoes,
That his troops sorely needed and could use.
On spotting Buford's cavalry approaching, he quickly
withdrew,

Having no orders to stand nor pursue.

Pettigrew told his commanding officer, General Heth,
   what he had seen,

But, neither Heth nor A.P. Hill believed the Union
   forces were so close to the scene.

General Heth now asked permission of General A.P. Hill
   to enter Gettysburg and procure those shoes from
   the nearby mill.

On July first, at five A.M., Heth's divisions coming down
   the Chambersburg Pike,

Were spotted by the Union cavalry and General Buford
   got ready for the fight.

He requested aid from Major General Reynolds's First
   Corps,

As he was badly outnumbered and the brunt of the
   battle bore.

Reynolds finally appeared on the scene,

As the Federal troops were driven across Willoughby
   Run, a very small stream.

Reynolds advised Buford to hold out, as more help was
   on the way

And informed General Meade that the Southern Troops,
   in force, were entering the fray.

Major General Reynolds was determined to hold
   Gettysburg at all costs,

And ordered Brigadier General Wadsworth's division to
   advance towards Gettysburg else all was lost.

General Doubleday, of baseball fame, was to bring the
   rest of the First Corps,

Followed by the Eleventh and Twelfth Corps to
   reinforce the engaging troops and even the score.

The fighting at McPherson's Ridge and Woods was hot
   and heavy,

As both the Blue and Gray endeavored to hold their
lines both firm and steady.
Brigadier General Archer, warned by Pettigrew to be
cautious,
Disregarded this sound advice and recklessly advanced
through McPherson's Woods where the fighting was
most ferocious.
The Nineteenth Indiana and the Twenty-fourth
Michigan turned Archer's right flank
And from the front and flanks, he was caught in a
murderous enfilade.
He was subsequently captured by the Iron Brigade
Of the Second Wisconsin Division, and the rest across
Willoughby Run made their escapade.
Many were captured in the battle that had just begun
As Archer's men were simply overrun.
At the other end of the line, the South had better
success
As Wadsworth and Cutler's men gave ground before
their determined aggressiveness.
Reynolds, urging the Iron Brigade on, was shot in the
head,
Fell off his horse, and on the battlefield lay dead.
General Meade approved of Reynolds's decision to hold
Gettysburg at all cost
And held him in high esteem, and the admiration of his
men was not lost.
He was born in nearby Lancaster, and Pennsylvania
was his home state
And to die on the field of battle, near his home, was his
fate.
Doubleday, Howard, and Hancock now assumed
command,

And each, as fortune decreed, contributed their skill as
    they made their stand.
Reinforcements were now arriving on all sides
As Ewell, deep in Pennsylvania, ordered Early and
    Rodes to Gettysburg to stem the tide.
Longstreet was still a day's journey away
And General Meade, still south of Gettysburg, was
    planning how to save the day.
Rodes, now, commenced his attack and some of his
    brigades met with some success,
But, those Southern brigades of O'Neil and Iverson
    were under great stress and duress,
And gave way as General Baxter stemmed the fray,
But the North Carolinians fought hard and brilliantly
    throughout the day.
General Lee, now, appeared on the scene
And, from the heights of Herr's Ridge, approved of what
    he had seen.
Jubal Early now reached the front
And General Barlow soon bore the brunt,
As both Rodes and Early assailed the Federal right
And were sweeping everything before them in the fight.
Barlow was severely wounded, but did survive,
As the units of the Eleventh Corps through the streets
    of Gettysburg retreated to stay alive.
At McPherson's Ridge, Pettigrew took command
As Heth was wounded and could not even stand.
The Twenty-sixth North Carolinian, Pettigrew put into
    action,
And yelling like demons charged the Iron Brigade in
    perfect formation.
The fighting was terrible as both sides stood their
    ground
And volley after volley their mark found.

The color-bearers of the Twenty-sixth North Carolinians
	particulaily were hard hit,
Having lost fourteen color-bearers including Privates,
	Captains, and Lieutenant Colonels who all bit the
	dirt.
Despite these losses to the South, the First Corps
	grudgingly gave ground
And made a final stand on Seminary Ridge and mound,
But, Major General Pender's crack divisions smashed
	the Blue
As bullets, shells, splinters, and carnage all around flew
And through the streets of Gettysburg, the First Corps,
	panic-stricken, spread.
Hancock and Howard, south of the town, set up
	defensive positions
And rallied the troops to turn around and face the
	opposition.
General Hancock, by Meade, was put in full command
Much to General Howard's chagrin, who was senior
	officer and didn't understand.
Nevertheless, they patched up their differences and
	went about their tasks.
And this was about all that anybody could possibly ask.
They immediately fortified the high ground
And stabilized the line south of the town.
General Hancock ordered General Doubleday to send
	part of the battered First Corps to Culp's Hill,
And General Doubleday complied and sent the battered
	Iron Brigade to fill the bill.
General Hancock ordered a defensive line on Cemetery
	Hill to be set up
And waited for reinforcements, who were on the way, to
	speed-up.

The line now extended from Culp's Hill and arched
    around Cemetery Hill,
Then along Cemetery Ridge to the base of Little Round
    Top, which was very still.
The line an inverted fish hook resembled;
And by crossing the arc, reinforcements could quickly be
    assembled.
By occupying the high grounds, Meade's hand was
    greatly strengthened,
And being able to reinforce any part of his line in a
    short period of time his outlook was greatly
    brightened.
Hancock, satisfied that his defensive line was now in
    place
And the panic-stricken troops were halted and turned
    about face,
Waited for reinforcements to arrive,
Hoping that they would come in time to save this
    disastrous day and survive.
The Union Army, by forced marches, towards
    Gettysburg streamed
As did the Southern Army marching up the
    Shenandoah Valley and their bayonets in the bright
    sun gleamed.
On Seminary Ridge, General Lee had his own troubled
    thoughts
As he surveyed the field that the day's end had brought.
General Longstreet finally arrived at the front
And his army was eager the North to confront.
Longstreet suggested that Lee sweep around Meade's
    left flank
And place himself between Meade's army and
    Washington, D.C. point blank.

Thus, Meade would have to attack the South from a defensive position.

Lee brushed aside this helpful suggestion.

Meade's Northern Army had close to 90,000 men all told,

And Lee had 70,000 men, all brave and bold.

Meade's Northern Army, from the South, was facing Lee

And Lee's Southern Army was facing Meade from the North: here was fate's irony.

General Lee, from Seminary Ridge, surveyed the field

And was happy at what he saw and determined not to yield.

He, too, recognized the advantage of possessing the high ground

And ordered A.P. Hill to renew his attack and the enemy pound,

But Hill declined, saying his troops were bloodied, weary, tired, and needed rest,

So Lee turned to Ewell and hoped for the best.

Ewell was gripped with mental inertia and couldn't make up his mind,

Whether to advance or just stay behind.

General Early and General Gordon urged Ewell to advance through the town

And seize the high hills and force a showdown.

Ewell maintained his orders were to come to Gettysburg and maintain his stand

And not to advance past Gettysburg to secure the land.

Brigadier General Trimble begged Ewell for permission to attack Culp's Hill,

But all his pleading and begging went for nil.

Trimble stomped away in rage

And was fit to be tied as a bird in a cage.

General Lee sent Major Taylor to Ewell's camp with
     orders to go on the attack,
But, the ambiguous order, "If practicable," puzzled
     Ewell and he held back.
Lee rode over to Ewell's headquarters to ascertain the
     delay
And wondered exactly what went astray.
By this time the sun was going down
And twilight was setting on the fields and town.
When Lee, at Ewell's headquarters, arrived,
All hopes of an attack were now deprived,
As General Slocum and General Sickle arrived in force
And a golden opportunity, to the South, was now lost.
Meade, from his headquarters in Tarrytown, now
     arrived and reviewed the site
And all his generals agreed that the topography was
     excellent for the coming fight.

The Second Day

July 2, 1863

General Lee, with only three hours of sleep, was up at
   3:30 A.M.
And from Seminary Ridge scanned the field and
   prepared his stratagem.
General Ewell held the town of Gettysburg, both to the
   south and to the north
A.P. Hill's troops faced Cemetery Hill and were ready to
   sally forth.
Longstreet's men were also almost at full might,
And were to the right of Hill's troops and were
   preparing for the fight.
The Southern Troops consisted of three divisions,
With Generals Ewell, A.P. Hill, and Longstreet
   commanding their respective positions.
Lieutenant General Ewell's division commanders were
   Rodes, Early, and Johnson.
A.P. Hill's commanders were Heth, Pender, and
   Anderson,
While Longstreet's were Pickett, McLaw, and Hood.
All division commanders were Major Generals and, in
   leadership, above average, stood.
The disposition of the Union forces were thus arrayed:
The battered First and Eleventh Corps on Cemetery
   Hill and Culp's Hill held sway.
They were supported by General Slocum and his
   Twelfth Corps,

And with the terrain in his favor, confidence was
    restored.
General Hancock was in charge of all the officers until
    General Meade would arrive,
Placed his Second Corps on Cemetery Hill and hoped
    the reinforcements would arrive in time to survive.
General Sickles and his Third Corps to the left of the
    Second Corps were arranged.
The Union line was three miles long and very little was
    changed.
It extended from Big and Little Round Top along
    Cemetery Ridge around Cemetery Hill, in an arc,
    and ended on Culp's Hill.
So on the morning of July second, everything was calm
    and everything was still.
From these defensive positions, General Meade and all
    his generals agreed
That they would attempt to stop the Confederate's
    attack and hoped that all would succeed.
General Sedgwick's Sixth Corps, by forced marches, up
    the Baltimore pike
Was streaming to Gettysburg, hoping to arrive in time
    for the fight.
General Lee made the following plans:
Longstreet was to attack Meade's left and drive the
    Federal Troops from Cemetery Ridge, if he can.
A.P. Hill would attack Cemetery Ridge from the west
And Ewell, at the sound of the first shots, would attack
Cemetery Hill and Culp's Hill and do his best.
The attack as planned by Lee was to be made in echelon
Starting at the right and proceeding to the left,
    squadron after squadron.
Thus, one brigade after another in a series of
    trip-hammer blows

Would strike the Union lines and in confusion the
    Union troops throw.
These orders were very complicated and split-second
    timing was needed for its success
Each division commander must be alert to ensure its
    progress.
These orders needed split-second timing to be
    synchronized to a tee
And all officers must be ready to improvise if the attack
    was to succeed.
Once again Longstreet urged Lee to outflank the Union
    lines,
But Lee will not heed this request and emphatically
    declines.
Lee ordered Longstreet at 10:00 A.M. to begin the
    attack,
And Lee was perturbed that Longstreet was holding
    back.
It wasn't until noon that Longstreet got under way
And the first of the trip-hammer blows came into play.
As Longstreet was getting his men in position,
Jeb Stuart finally arrived from his roundabout
    expedition.
He would be of no help to Lee on this day
As his cavalry was strung out and would not arrive
    before midday.
General Sickles and the Third Corps, not satisfied with
    the low terrain,
Advanced his forces to higher ground and thus a better
    position gain.
At 3:00 P.M. ten thousand men of the Third Corps' army
Advanced a half-mile beyond the Union line in splendid
    panoply.

Meade was furious at this advance and ordered Sickles
　　back to his original position,
But the sound of gunfire informed him it was too late to
　　rectify this condition.
Sickles's advance thwarted Lee's plan to roll up the
　　Union flank
Along Emmitsburg Road; McLaw protested vigorously
　　to commence the attack, but was outranked.
Thrice he urged Longstreet to alter his plans,
And thrice he was rebuked and told to follow Lee's
　　commands.
Hood, also, was faced with the same dilemma
And begged Longstreet to change the plans and agenda.
He, too, besieged Longstreet to change his mind,
But Longstreet told him to follow Lee's orders and so
　　declined.
(Officers, who are fighting in the front line,
Have a better perspective and should not strict orders
　　be confined.)
There was no way that Lee or Longstreet, who were in
　　the rear,
Could possibly see Sickles's Third Corps, suddenly, in
　　their front appear.
Hood disregarded Longstreet's orders and moved his
　　divisions eastward
And attacked Devil's Den and Big Round Top as he
　　moved forward;
The Alabama brigade, supported by the Georgian and
　　Texas brigade,
Up the steep slopes of Big Round Top, struggled to
　　invade.
The Fifteenth Alabama, under Colonel Oates, reached
　　the top,
305 feet above the plain, and secured Big Round Top.

He envisioned a few cannons there would play havoc
    with the Union forces
And could easily rake Cemetery Hill and Culp's Hill
    with very heavy losses.
He really believed that the answer to Gettysburg was in
    his hands,
But the gods of war thwarted his well-laid plans.
Hood was wounded and McLaw was now in command.
McLaw ordered Oates to abandon Big Round Top and
    his plan,
And attack Little Round Top
Immediately, with no stop.
Meade sent General Warren to Little Round Top to
    survey
And reconnoiter the situation and make his assay.
Immediately he recognized the importance of Little
    Round Top,
As Colonel Oates, just moments before, recognized the
    advantages of Big Round Top:
That whoever held the high ground
Was at an advantage, as for miles around,
The movement of troops could be seen and found.
Warren implored aid from whomever he could
And Colonel Vincent and his brigade answered the call
    and stood,
And hid behind rocks as Colonel Oates and his men
    appeared.
A scant ten minutes earlier and the South would have
    commandeered.
Colonel Chamberlain's Twentieth Maine Regiment was
    ordered at all costs
To hold their ground and give not an inch or the battle
    For Little Round Top would be lost.
The Confederates rushed up the hill,

But were met by a murderous fire and determined will.
They wavered and staggered back,
Reformed and regrouped and again advanced to the
    attack.
The air was filled with bullets and lead
As the Alabamians advanced over their wounded and
    dead.
Time and time again they rushed to the fore,
And time and time again, they were repulsed once
    more.
The fighting was furious and hand to hand
And shouts, cries, groans and curses rose over the land.
As the Confederates were regrouping for another
    charge,
Chamberlain, with ammunition running low, with fixed
    bayonets counter-charged.
The Confederates stopped, halted, and fell back,
And when fresh Federal Troops attacked his flanks,
    Oates called off the attack.
At the other end of the line, Vincent's Sixteenth
    Michigan Brigade,
Under the pounding of Robertson's Texas Brigade,
    began to falter and fade away.
As Colonel Vincent tried to rally his Michigan men,
He was mortally wounded and died in the hard-fought
    glen.
"Don't give an inch," were the last words he said
And gloom among the Michigan men was widespread.
While the battle raged below,
General Warren was helping Lieutenant Hazlett
    assemble his cannons on the hill and plateau.
Again Warren sent reinforcements just in time,
As he sent Colonel O'Rorke and his 140th New York,
    just as

The Texans were succeeding in their climb.
He reached Little Round Top, on the western slope,
And smashed into Robertson's Texans and deprived
    them of hope.
Unfortunately, while leading the charge, he was killed
And died defending the now famous hill.
When General Weed, Paddy O'Rorke's superior, heard
    of O'Rorke heading for Little Round Top,
Turned his three regiments around and headed there
    without a stop.
He arrived when the action had all but ceased,
But, sniper fire was now on the increase,
And General Weed was hit by a minee ball
And requested Lieutenant Hazlett to heed his call.
As Hazlett leaned over to hear what he had to say,
He, too, was struck in the head and immediately passed
    away.
General Warren had now saved the day,
With his timely infusion of reinforcements into the fray.
While the struggle for Little Round Top was on its way,
Hood's other divisions, around Devil's Den and Plum
    Run, came into play.
Here the heaviest fighting for Gettysburg was fought
And many men, both Blue and Gray, found here their
    final resting place that Fate had sought.
Robertson's Texas and Arkansas, and Benning's
    Georgians' Brigades, all under General McLaw,
Attacked Devil's Den and Plum Run, and the battle
    back and forth see-sawed.
Devil's Den—a Godforsaken place—with huge boulders
    and rocks,
The Blue and the Gray in mortal battle lock.
Charges and counter-charges were the order of the day

20

As on the opposite side of the same boulder, men flared
    away.
Plum Run, "The Valley of Death," as it was afterwards
    known,
Was with the dead, wounded, and maimed completely
    sown.
Every man was his own general and gave orders,
But, no one paid any heed to them in the ensuing fury
    and disorder.
The second of the trip-hammer blows began to unfold,
As Hood's divisions under Anderson and Benning
    charged ahead to gain a foothold.
General Birney's thin line bore the brunt of the attack
As the Southerners kept coming and refused to fall
    back.
De Trobriand, a French Aristocrat, held his line intact
And thwarted the Southern boys in their very act.
When General Barnes, fighting in the Peach Orchard,
    retreated to a more favorable position,
He exposed De Trobriand's right flank to a dangerous
    condition.
With his right flank exposed, De Trobriand was forced
    to give way,
Suffering heavy losses as the Gray streamed across the
    Wheat Fields and almost carried the day.
General Hancock sent General Caldwell with fresh
    troops into the fray,
And on the double-quick, fired and charged into the
    mad melee.
The first of Caldwell's brigade to arrive, was Colonel
    Cross,
Who, with his men, eagerly charged to stem the loss.
Ten minutes later he was fatally wounded
And died that night greatly lamented.

Next, Brigadier General Zook entered the fray
But found his way barred by Barnes's men, who were
    retreating in disarray.
Zook was enraged and shouted, "If you can't get out of
    the way,
Lie down and we will march over you," so eager was he
    to save the day.
To the astonishment of all, they did lie down
And over the prone bodies his troops charged into the
    Wheat Field for a showdown.
Zook was among the first to fall;
As his horse leaped over a stone wall, a bullet ended it
    all.
Next, Colonel Patrick Kelly's Irish Brigade appeared on
    the scene
And plugged the gap between Cross's troops and Zook's
    as they intervene.
Finally, General Coldwell threw in his last brigade,
Under Colonel Booke, who charged and the Wheat Field
    did invade.
General Semmes's Georgian troops slowed, stopped, and
    gave ground,
But not for long for they regrouped, and reinforced,
    charged into the swirling compound.
The Wheat Field changed hands for the sixth time,
As both the Blue and Gray charged and counter-charged
    to possess this ground of bloody slime.
While the fighting in the Wheat Field was taking its
    bloody toll,
An attack in the Peach Orchard was about to unfold.
General McLaw ordered General Barksdale and his
    Mississippi Brigade
Into the Peach Orchard to advance and invade.

General Barksdale, a barrel-chested former
   Congressman,
Had a thirst for battle glory
And begged McLaw and Longstreet to enter the fray
   without further dilatory.
When McLaw finally ordered him to advance,
His face lit up with joy and he entered the battle with
   great vengeance.
"Forward, men, forward," he shouted over and over
   again,
As his Mississippians smashed General Graham's
   Federal line,
Who broke and gave ground under the bright sunshine.
General Graham was wounded and taken captive.
The Third Corps line was broken and General Graham's
   division was rendered inoffensive.
This exposed the flank of Caldwell's forces in the Wheat
   Field,
And General Wofford's Georgians pushed the Federals
   back and forced them to also yield.
General Sickles, the Third Corps commander, had his
   leg severed in the battle
And was carried off the field puffing on a Havana cigar
   like a Roman candle.
Most of the Third Corps' divisions were badly mauled
   and in full retreat,
But General Humphrey's divisions would not admit
   defeat.
They retreated, fighting fiercely as they gave ground.
And reached Cemetery Ridge with its friendly
   compound.
It was now A.P. Hill's corps's turn to continue the
   trip-hammer blows

And General Anderson sent Wilcox and Lane's divisions
    against the foe.
Twenty times Humphrey halted his men and faced
    about,
Firing on the foe and preventing a rout.
Finally the survivors reached Hancock's Second Corps,
On Cemetery Ridge, where Hancock did yeoman work
    and helped order to restore.
He was in complete command and juggled his forces
By sending reinforcements, wherever needed, to lessen
    his losses.
General Meade, from his inner hooked-shaped line,
Also sent reinforcements to Little Round Top to save
    this important life-line.
They arrived just in time as the Gray broke through the
    Wheat Field.
And headed straight for Little Round Top, determined
    not to yield.
They were met by a Pennsylvania reserve division
    charging down the hill
And drove the Confederates back to the Wheat Field
    with great pluck and skill.
The Twelfth Corps, from Culp's Hill, ran cross-country
    towards the sound of gunfire,
And did all they could to stem the quagmire.
The First Corps, under Generals Doubleday and
    Robinson,
Though badly battered the previous day, rushed into
    the cauldron
From their positions, behind Cemetery Hill,
And helped stem the tide with determined will.
Three brigades, under General Sedgwick, though
    exhausted from their all-night plight,
Were thrown into the breech to join the fight.

Two more brigades of General Anderson, now, entered
    the fray,
Under Brigadier General Wright and straight for
    Cemetery Ridge made their way.
Meanwhile, Barksdale, sweeping through the Peach
    Orchard after hard fighting,
Met stiff opposition from McGilvery's Maine and
    Bigelow's Massachusetts artillery and bombing.
They slowed the Mississippians down but did not stop
    them.
(Artillery pieces without infantry support is no
    stratagem.)
Again timely reinforcements saved the day
As Burling's brigade and Willard's, led by General
    Hancock, himself, rushed into the fray.
Willard was decapitated by a shell, but Barksdale's
    men, still began to fall back.
They disputed every inch of ground and neither will nor
    courage lacked.
While trying to rally his men, Barksdale was wounded
    fatally
And his men gave ground and fell back grudgingly.
As Barksdale's men retreated, General Hancock saw
    more trouble to the north,
He ordered Gibbon's and Hay's divisions to sally forth
And confront Cadmus Wilcox's brigade as they charged
    an open gap on Cemetery Ridge.
General Hancock knew that Wilcox would reach the gap
    before aid could come to stop the surge.
A five-minute delay was all Hancock needed
To thwart Wilcox's charge before it succeeded.
Hancock spotted a regiment that stood on Cemetery
    Ridge behind an artillery battery.

He galloped towards them shouting, "What regiment is this?" in his urgency.

"The First Minnesota," Colonel Colvill shouted back.

Hancock asked, "Colonel, do you see those colors in front of the pack?"

Colvill nodded. "Then take them!" ordered General Hancock.

The First Minnesota with fixed bayonets absorbed the shock,

One undersized regiment against an entire brigade.

The 262 Minnesotans fearlessly flung themselves at Wilcox's brigade in a noble crusade.

Only 47 men fit for combat remained,

But five minutes or more were gained.

Gibbon's men soon arrived and poured a murderous fire on Wilcox's men,

Who were hard pressed to stem the tide and their ground defend.

Wilcox's brigade stalled and he asked General Anderson for help and aid,

But, no attention to his frantic plea for help was paid.

Wilcox had no choice but to order a retreat,

As did Lang with his small Florida brigade, to avert utter defeat.

General Wright, with the retreat of these two brigades, exposed both his flanks,

And he was sorely pressed to maintain order in his ranks.

He was still pounding the center of Cemetery Ridge with some success.

He was all alone, a mile in front of Lee's armies, but still made progress.

Brigadier General Webb and his men a murderous fire on the Gray sent.

As happened, time and time again, timely Union
      reinforcements
Arrive and death and destruction on the Gray vent.
Doubleday and Robinson's forces together with Webb's
Surround Wright's Georgian Brigade in a very close
      web.
Wright ordered his men to cut their way out and retreat
Or all would have to surrender and suffer defeat.
Wright to his dying day, firmly believed, if reinforced,
He'd have broken through the center of Cemetery Ridge
      and would not have lost.
On Wright's left, the Confederate troops of Posey
      refused to attack
And the trip-hammer blows that Lee had envisioned
      were held back.
General Mahone, who was next in line to proceed,
Took his cue from Posey and refused to intercede.
General Pender, next in line to attack, rode over to
      Mahone to ascertain the delay
When he was mortally wounded and was removed from
      the fray.
Had he lived he would no doubt have joined the
      charge—
He was very aggressive—even though Mahone refused
      to barge.
Lee firmly believed if Pender on his horse for another
      half-hour, had remained,
The battle of Gettysburg would have been won and
      victory attained.
Mahone, even after Anderson ordered him to advance,
Remained adamantly inactive and refused to change his
      stance.
Anderson, A.P. Hill, and even Lee, himself, must
      shoulder the blame

For the timely help that never came.
Split-second decisions and timing were needed in this
      complicated attack,
And all were lacking and contributed to this setback.
The Blue, time and time again, strengthened their lines
      with timely reinforcements,
Whenever the Gray appeared to be breaking through,
      and thus victory prevent.
Meanwhile, General Ewell, on the extreme left of the
      Confederate forces, had orders from Lee
To attack the Union lines as soon as he heard
      Longstreet's artillery.
He was to attack Culp's Hill and Cemetery Hill and the
      Union forces pin down,
Thus affording Longstreet and Hill to succeed without
      help being brought from across town.
Most of the Union units on Culp's Hill and one-half
      from Cemetery Hill
Had gone to reinforce the line against Longstreet and
      Hill.
For two hours, while Longstreet and Hill's divisions
      were battering themselves in bloody eradication,
Ewell withered away the morning, noon, and afternoon
      hours in inexcusable hesitation.
His men, under the hot sun, chaffed and grew restless
And wondered if they would ever see action before the
      coming darkness.
With the attack on all fronts now silent,
Ewell decided to commence his attack on his salient.
It was the most inopportune time to commence this
      surge
As darkness was falling fast and no advantage to Lee
      could possibly emerge.
General Meade, probably, could not have cared less,

For he had the whole Union Army to come to their
    defense.
Lack of synchronized attacks was costly to Lee,
Although the South fought with courage and gallantry;
The top leadership bordered on mediocrity.
Johnson's three divisions commenced their attack
On Culp's Hill, but the North held and didn't fall back.
Jubal Early was to advance to Cemetery Hill
With Rodes's forces to come in and complete the kill.
As happened throughout the whole day,
Union reinforcements kept arriving to stem the fray.
General Hay's Louisiana Tigers had great success
And captured Rickett's cannons and made great
    progress.
Again General Hancock sent aid just in time,
And sent Carroll and his men to stem the Louisiana
    Tigers in their climb.
The Louisiana Tigers, outflanked, scrambled back down
    on Cemetery Hill,
And Ewell's late attack ended in the quiet evening still.
Rodes was tardy in getting his men into the fight,
And when he was ready, Early and Johnson were done
    for the night.
At midnight, Meade called a council of war,
And all agreed to hold their ground as they had done
    before.
The South held the Peach Orchard, the Wheat Field,
    Devil's Den and Plum Run,
While the North held on to Little Round Top, the key to
    Gettysburg, which they had won.
Night slumbered over the whole battleground,
And the cries of the wounded were the only sound.

Lee prepared his final strategy for the next day
And astonished the world as his panoramic and daring
    plan unfolded and came into play.

The Third Day

Pickett's Charge

July 3, 1863

Phoebus Apollo scanned the sky
On that fateful day of the third of July
As he drives his golden chariot in the early morn,
And ushers in Homer's "rosy-fingered dawn."
The little town of Gettysburg he sees below
As two mighty armies prepare for the final blow.
Lee, with his gallant and chivalrous band,
And Meade, with the mighty Potamic Army, stand
And face each other and the respect of all command.
The fate of the nation is in their hands
And on their strength of arms, the verdict stands.
General Lee, with his valiant boys,
Surveys the field and with victory toys.
General Meade, with his veteran troops, await
Across the fields and contemplate their fate.
Lee had attacked Meade's flanks both left and right,
And now he was determined to attack Meade's center
    with all his might.
Pickett's men, just newly arrived, would lead the
    charge,
Supported by A.P. Hill's divisions and victory loomed
    large.
The battle plans were now laid out
And Pickett's three divisions would start the bout.

On Pickett's left, Hill's divisions, under Pettigrew, held sway

And to their rear, Scale's and Lane's brigades made their way.

Lane's and Scale's brigades were under the command of General Trimble, of Maryland.

Brave Colonel Fry, the Tennessee brigade, led and scanned,

And with Pettigrew, the front lines manned.

Mayo's troops supported the flanks of General Pettigrew,

And all comprised a most valiant crew.

To the right, to protect the flanks of Pickett, the crew

Of Wilcox and Perry maneuvered to their rendezvous.

All morning long the troops sweltered in the heat

As they awaited the orders to charge and the enemy defeat.

Lee planned the charge for early morn,

With Ewell to attack Meade's right at dawn.

Simultaneously, Pickett was to charge over the open fields

And force Meade's center to bend and yield.

But the Gods of War had other plans

That would void the designs even of an Olympian.

Unfortunately, Meade's right flank attacked Ewell's troops

And thwarted Lee's plans before Pickett's men were even grouped.

For six long hours, the battle was fought.

As Longstreet dragged his feet and Lee's patience grew short.

Longstreet's heart wasn't in the attack

And thought the charge over open fields lacked tact.

All morning long, while the attack was going on, Lee
     fumed
Because his orders to Longstreet to charge had not even
     loomed.
By eleven o'clock Ewell's attack was spent
And Pickett's men under the hot sun remained diligent.
A golden opportunity was now beyond retrieve
Because it freed Meade's men to rest and relieve.
Suddenly, at one o'clock all hell broke loose
As 120 cannons all along the line death and destruction
     produced.
The North answered with a volley of their own,
And equal death and destruction on the Southern lines
     were sown.
For two long hours the cannonade lasts,
But the two sides their prearranged positions held fast.
The Union cannons slacked their fire
And saved their ammunition for the charge they knew
     would surely transpire.
General Alexander mistook this lull, thought his
     cannons had taken their toll
And beckoned Pickett to commence his charge and goal.
Pickett asked General Longstreet if he should advance
     his guard,
And Longstreet, with a heavy heart and reluctant to
     speak, just gave a lazy nod.
Forward! Guide center! March! the order came
And out of the woods, the men of the South the open
     field claim.
Pickett's charge had now begun
And once started couldn't be undone.
The die was cast! The Rubicon had been crossed!
And into the jaws of death the troops were tossed.

In three straight lines, one-half mile long, in
    magnificent array
At shoulder arms with determined step, they made
    their way
And across the fields their discipline display
As the hope of the South with these valiant boys lay.
Nine brigades made the charge; twelve thousand men
    all told
From Virginia, Tennessee, North Carolina, Alabama,
    and Mississippi, all brave and bold.
Even the Union Army at this brilliant display
Marveled at the courage of the Southern boys dressed in
    Gray.
For more than a half mile, they charged over open
    fields,
Nothing to shield them but their own hearts of steel.
The Union cannons opened up on the Southern troops.
But their ranks neither paused, faltered, nor drooped.
Shells fell before them, behind, and amongst them,
But their lines held fast to their stratagem.
Frightful gaps were made in the center and flanks,
But Pickett's boys steadily advanced and closed their
    ranks.
"Left Oblique!" the command was now conveyed,
And Pickett's Virginians immediately the order obeyed.
When the lines joined Pettigrew's troops,
The ranks were united in one solid group.
Stannard and his Vermont boys, this maneuver saw
And at right angles to Kemper's men, his boys bore;
A murderous fire into Kemper's troops he poured.
So intent were the Virginians to reach the Union lines
    that this fire was ignored.
The cannons on Little Round Top and Cemetery Hill
    took their toll,

But the brave Virginians did not fold.
On the left flank, Mayo's troops by the Eighth Ohioans
    were defeated.
This exposed the flanks of Pettigrew, and Davis's
    brigade began to crumble.
Pettigrew's other brigades and the Virginians did not
    stumble
But maintained their deliberate pace and held their
    fire,
As the Confederate forces fast reaching Cemetery
    Ridge, was their one desire.
Pettigrew's left flank remained unprotected
And a withering cannon fire on his troops was detected.
Pettigrew's right continued in good order on its way,
Led by the brave Tennesseans and North Carolinians
    who never wavered in the fray,
But fought as long, bled as much, and fell as fast as the
    Virginians on that day.
Both the Blue and the Gray superhuman courage
    display
As only death and destruction before them lay,
As the gods above the fate of every man assay.
"Front Forward!" came the command and cry
And Pickett's charging boys on the double-quick did fly.
Wilcox and Perry now commenced their attack,
But, again Stannard poured volley after volley and
    forced them back.
Pickett's Virginians reached the center, at the now
    famous angle,
And with Fry's Tennesseans with the foe began to
    tangle.
They leaped over stone walls in small groups
And pierced and sent reeling the Union Troops.
The fighting was fierce, savage, and hand to hand,

Cursing, hollering and shooting whatever the situation
    demand.
Garnett, leading his brigade in the charge, went down
And only his bloodied horse was ever found.
Kemper was shot and crippled for life;
Only Armistead was left to command the strife.
With his hat on his sword, he charged into the Union
    mass
And reached the cannons, but his men fell fast.
He too, at last received a mortal blow
And to the last, he lashed his sword at the oncoming
    foe.
Also wounded in battle were Pettigrew and Fry,
And Trimble lost a leg as the enemy defy.
Cushing's as well as Brown's Rhode Island batteries
    were destroyed,
New cannons were rushed up and deployed.
Union reinforcements at the angle, on the double-quick
    were rushed,
And the Confederate hopes were all but crushed.
Hancock, Gibbons, Hays and Webb do ride
And like raging bulls try to stem the tide.
Devereux with the Nineteenth Massachusetts and
    Forty-second New York were rushed to the breech
To help stem the tide that the Confederates had
    reached.
The Seventy-second Pennsylvanian rushed in to stem
    the flow.
The Sixty-ninth Pennsylvania reeled and wavered from
    the blow.
With cannon fire taking a deadly toll on their center
    and flanks
And musket fire depleting their ranks,
They looked behind them and saw no help was there

And soon Pickett's lines crumbled and fled and gave up
 in despair
It seemed like a miracle, indeed, that any of them ever
 reached the Union lines
And realized that to have pierced the center, even for a
 moment, the law of war defies.
To those who were in the charge and died or lived to tell
 the story,
To them, indeed, remains the honor of long and
 everlasting glory!
Pickett now knew that all was lost
And wheeled his horse around and left the holocaust.
Phoebus Apollo circled the heavens and ended this day
With tears in his eyes for both the Blue and the Gray.

Epilogue

The sun's rays irradiated over the great battlefield
And the grass below the scars of war have healed.
North and South together now, hand in hand,
Were soon to become one nation
And peace would reign over the land.
And brother and brother, with arms entwined,
Along the winding road elusive peace did find.
And the nation again renewed its day
And on to glory made its way.
And ever upwards, O Union, pursue thy fate
And never falter, halt nor wait,
But thrust your energies to the stars; to reach and to
    hold
And to the whole world its mysteries unfold.
Then hold your beacon high and its bright light unfurl
And with renewed strength enlighten the World!

Appendix: The Gettysburg Address

November 19, 1863

"Fourscore and seven years ago our fathers brought forth on this continent a new nation, conceived in liberty and dedicated to the proposition that all men are created equal. Now we are engaged in a great civil war, testing whether that nation or any nation so conceived and so dedicated can long endure. We are met on a great battle-field of that war. We have come to dedicate a portion of that field as a final resting-place for those who here gave their lives that that nation might live. It is altogether fitting and proper that we should do this. But in a larger sense, we cannot dedicate, we cannot consecrate, we cannot hallow this ground. The brave men, living and dead who struggled here have consecrated it far above our poor power to add or detract. The world will little note nor long remember what we say here, but it can never forget what they did here. It is for us the living rather to be dedicated here to the unfinished work which they who fought here have thus far so nobly advanced. It is rather for us to be here dedicated to the great task remaining before us—that from these honored dead we take increased devotion to that cause for which they gave the last full measure of devotion—that we here highly resolve that these dead shall not have died in vain, that this nation under God shall have a new birth of freedom, and that government of the people, by the people, for the people shall not perish from the earth."